BRIDGE

Define, Build, & Ignite the Life of Your Dreams

SCOTT ROWLEY

PUBLISHED BY PEAK PROSPER, INC.
HOOD RIVER, OREGON, USA

This book was written to guide you on the path to realizing the life of your dreams.

The advice and ideas presented in this book are not intended to replace help from your physician or healthcare provider. In matters relating to your health, you should consult a medical professional, especially if you have preexisting conditions.

BRIDGE: Define, Build, and Ignite the Life of Your Dreams.

Published by Peak Prosper, Inc.

Please contact info@peakprosper.com for bulk order purchases.

1st Edition: October 2018

Table of Contents

ACKNOWLEDGMENTS

A sincere thank you to all who helped make this book project a reality: my family, friends, mentors, doctors, editor, business partner, and guiding Spirit.

Your unwavering love, direction, and inspiration continue to fuel me during each step of the journey.

And a huge heartfelt sense of gratitude to the global audience that I get to share this work with.

Keep climbing one step closer to the life of your dreams, and when you get there, soak it in, and keep living it.

Summit as Friends,
Scott

PREFACE

Step.

Breathe.

It was all I could do to keep moving.

My body hurt so bad as a result of the last 24-hours.

And it was not the first time, but God willing it would be the last.

Death had washed over me.

I felt like my heart was going to pound out of my chest, or my body was going to stop functioning in the middle of the woods.

I'd spent the last 24-hours consuming alcohol, cocaine, marijuana, and bad food—all poison.

And, finally, I had reached a diverging point on the trail of my life. At that moment, I realized that I could continue in the direction I was heading, or dive headfirst into a transformational change.

I'd found a new bottom, and it was there that I could rebuild my bed-rock so living the life I'd always dreamed of would become possible.

Up to this moment, I'd built a pretty successful life on the outside, filled with the completion of dozens of marathons, skiing all over the globe, building several businesses, climbing mountains, developing a successful corporate career, and being an active member of my community.

But the truth, through all of this, I was dying on the inside. Always seeking more external fulfillment; "enough" never existed. And there-fore, I would go through continuous cycles of building my life back, breaking it down, rinsing and repeating this over and over again.

Unpleasant transformations began to settle into my mind, body, and spirit, like depression, loneliness, and sickness. Every day was worse than the last. And every day got harder to do the simplest things, like get out of bed in the morning, get dressed, and get moving.

Until that day, I showed up at the Tamanawas trailhead for a short hike with my mother, and each step and breath also became harder than the last. On that hike, I realized that everything had to start changing, or I would die quickly as a result of the lifestyle I'd built.

Life had to change, not in a day or two, or week or three.

It had to change today.

IT ALL CHANGES

Since that day, everything has changed.

My career, how I live, what I do on a day-to-day basis.

I emptied every physical, emotional, and spiritual drawer in my life looked at it and decided if it was something I wanted to keep or not.

Today, I don't drink alcohol or use drugs in any form, and I strive to live in alignment with my life purpose:

To use my adventurous spirit and passion for personal excellence to inspire and empower people all over the world.

This book is the detailed process I have gone through that has empowered me with the strength to stop running from my problems, and to start taking ownership over every aspect of my life resulting in living my dreams.

My life is still far from perfect. Some days, I run into physical, emotional, and spiritual walls, but these make me stronger because I do not quit.

I find a way to push through, climb over, or break the walls down.

I keep surrendering to the process and, when necessary, fighting for what I have come to believe is the right thing: to live simply and to share each word and action from a state of compassion, love, and stillness.

I feel blessed to get to share this work with you, and while there were many other pieces to my complex puzzle, the components shared here will surely help you on your path to living the life of your dreams.

The ideas, frameworks, and exercises in this book require that you read with an open mind, do the work, and embrace a beautiful change that is already growing within you.

May each step of your journey bring you joy.

Laugh a lot, do not take yourself too seriously, and keep moving forward one word, breath, and exercise at a time.

INTRODUCTION

"You cannot start writing your next chapter of life if you keep re-reading the last one."

Now is the time to ignite the life you have always imagined and to start living each day in alignment with the purpose that brings you daily joy.

Welcome to the starting line—the early mornings, planning, hard work, and next steps on your journey to living the life of your dreams.

WHAT TO EXPECT

This book is intended to guide you into a natural, healthy rhythm of enjoying new experiences, living life on purpose, and contributing to the betterment of our world as a result of doing the work you love.

You will find that parts of the book become daily, weekly, monthly, and annual reference points as you flow through life and the changes that inevitably await behind each corner.

ENJOY THE CHANGE

As you journey through this book, you will begin to feel a new you coming to life. Your dreams and wishes will start to be translated into the real daily life you get to live, no matter how big or small they are.

Find joy in this journey, and you will have discovered an ultimate form of success.

ACTIVE LEARNING EXPERIENCE

The book format integrates an active learning style by creating or seeing a vivid image of what you are learning, reading just enough to go out and apply it, and finally journaling about your experience so you can share it with others.

This multi-level approach to learning helps turn something into a habit, delivering more sustainable and positive results in the long run compared to just trying something for a short period, then slipping back into our old ways of being.

Please take these activities to heart as they are where you will experience the real change that translates what were once dreams into reality.

FEAR OF CHANGE

Undeniably, change can be hard. However, it is an inevitable fact of life. It provides a beautiful opportunity for us to create a happier, healthier, more inspiring "us," and requires that we take 100% ownership of all aspects of our lives, so we can shape them around what brings us the most joy.

If you sit in fear of massive change in this very moment as I did for years, then take a deep breath, believe you are right where you need to be in this moment, and lean into the process that is laid out in the pages that follow.

FLOW

I use the word "flow" many times throughout the book, as this is one of the most important lessons that I can share. When you read this word, use it as a reminder that flow is now.

Flow is a state of mind that you will find as a result of being so immersed in what you are doing that energy, and focus naturally gains momentum with each continued action. It is a mental, physical, and spiritual state of complete presence that we all have at our fingertips right now.

LET'S BEGIN

Your new journey into self-discovery has already begun.

Right now is your window of opportunity to take massive action that will empower you with transformational experiences.

Act on your current inspiration, do not delay and let's build your solid bedrock which will become the foundation for creating the life of your dreams.

PART ONE:

BUILD A SOLID BEDROCK

CHAPTER 1

BREATHE

"Breathing is the first step to energizing our dreams, settling our minds, and welcoming a new moment of life."

BREATHING, YUP, JUST BREATHE

At this moment, right now, you do not need to do anything but breathe.

Before you begin, take a moment to focus on your breath.

Inhale. Exhale.

And repeat the flow as you read on.

Breathing provides moments of pause that open our minds up to life's necessities and new opportunities that we may have never imagined.

Clean, fresh air flowing rhythmically in and out of our bodies delivers positive, focused energy that relieves us from anxiety and tension.

Now, smile into your next breath of life.

A new journey has begun, and breathing will be a source of fuel to keep you going each step of the way.

FOCUS THROUGH BREATH

Breathing helps bring you focus by nourishing your mind, body, and spirit.

It helps you see when your mind is racing with too many thoughts. So many that everything is like a whiteout on a mountain.

Breathing has the power to calm the storm in your mind so you can adequately channel all your energy in the right direction.

When you feel your mind begin racing, slow it down a little with a few deep breaths.

JUST TAKE A MOMENT TO BREATHE

Inhale, feel your whole body filling up with positive energy.

Exhale, feel the distractions and tension float away.

Pause, feel your body begin starving for more air.

Hear and feel your heartbeat, environment, and movements as you breathe.

What do you hear?

What do you feel?

Keep breathing.

CLEAN VS. TOXIC AIR

Smell the air as it fills your body.

What do you smell?

Good, clean, fresh air? Dirty toxins? Or nothing at all?

The odor of your environment can tell you a lot about whether you are fueling your body or causing life-threatening damage.

As you exhale, connect with how that breath makes you feel.

Do you feel settled?

Calm?

Energized?

Focused?

Or, do you feel tired, drowsy, nervous, unstable?

Do you feel like you're still starving for air?

A BREATHING PRACTICE FOR ANYTIME OF DAY

Box breathing is a simple yet powerful practice that can be used throughout your day to bring more ease to each moment, and it only takes a few minutes. As a result of this practice, you will improve your mood, performance, focus, and overall wellbeing in a matter of minutes.

Use this tool before meetings, between chores, and when your mind is stuck in a state of thinking.

ACTIVITY 1.1: Inspire Your Life With Box Breathing
TIME: 3 Minutes
SUMMARY:

- Get settled in an environment with clean air (e.g., nature, a city park, inside a well-filtered room with plants, or right where you are in this moment).
- If you are inside, then take a few minutes to clean up your space.
- Move into a comfortable seated or standing position.
- Complete a scan of your entire body, looking for areas of tension. Mentally connect with this tension and physically let it go.
- Complete 4 Rounds of Box Breathing
  - Inhale through your nose for 4 seconds.
  - Hold your breath for 4 seconds.
  - Exhale through your mouth for 4 seconds.
  - Hold your breath for 4 seconds.
  - Repeat the box breathing cycle until you feel grounded, clear-minded, and energized.
- Return to this activity whenever you feel the need to settle your mind or inspire your life with new energy.

CHAPTER 2

AWAKEN YOUR DREAMS

"Don't let your dreams lie dormant. Share them, write them, work during the day and dream at night about them, and before you know it, you will be living them."

BELIEVE IN A LIFE FULL OF MIRACLES

Whoever said dreams never come true did not dare to believe, take action, and dream like a kid again.

What have you always wanted to experience, be, and have in life?

At some point, did you stop believing that your wildest dreams were possible?

Never stop believing that a miracle is going to happen because the next miracle might be what you need to turn what was a dream into your reality.

WHAT IS A DREAM?

A dream is no more than a conscious or subconscious thought we experience while sleeping or awake that is yet to be realized.

Your dreams do have the ability to come true, so long as you resurface them, make a realistic plan, and make consistent daily progress.

CONSISTENT REST INSPIRES DREAMS

Accessing your deepest desires that will bring life fulfillment is supported by having a consistent sleep pattern. While everyone's sleep routine is a little different, the average person needs 8-9 hours of sleep each night to allow the body time for recovery before your next day's push. Whatever time you lie down at night, be sure to schedule 8-9 hours for rest to inspire clear thoughts the following day.

Additionally, scheduling a few short naps throughout the day allows you the opportunity to recharge your brain and body function resulting in richer experiences and higher quality work. These short naps often spark vivid thoughts and ideas that you will remember for a short time upon awakening which is a great reason to have a dream notebook at the ready.

GOOD VS. EVIL DREAMS

Not all visions we experience are good. Many of them could be evil.

They might tell us we are not enough, and attempt to shatter our positive images that paint the life of our happy future.

Embrace these evil thoughts, then let them go. Remind yourself that they are nothing more than bad thoughts trying to act against you. Deflate them them by focusing on what you most desire.

Let them float away like a feather in the wind. Remind yourself that you are healthy and courageous, that you can and will win the fight against the negative voice in your head.

And always remember to smile, because evil thoughts and ideas just cannot handle positive emotion.

Welcome your positive thoughts, ideas, and emotions. Write them down, share them with others, and act upon them.

IT ALL STARTS AS A DREAM

Breathe in.

Let go.

Smile.

And always remember,

that just because we age,

our dreams needn't die.

For this is when our dreams should most thrive,

now is the time to breathe in and bring your dreams alive.

Share them for the world to see,

including dreamers just like me.

And, in sharing our dreams, we take the first step,

so simple it may seem,

this book itself was at first but a dream.

SHARE YOUR DREAM

Once you have found that vivid picture of what your heart most desires, share it with the world, whatever you do, do not keep it locked up inside. Let it free so it may become your reality.

Your dreams were never meant to be locked up inside of you. Good or bad, share them, write about them, talk about them, and if you want them bad enough, take action so you may realize them.

CONNECTING YOUR DREAMS TO REALITY

Dreams are merely visions experienced during sleep or waking moments that represent something different than here and now. Sometimes they are places we wish to go, experiences we would love to have, or the contrary: nightmares, things we wish would never happen to us.

They are nothing more than vivid thoughts or ideas, but this is where all great things are first born.

The first step to turning a dream into a reality is to gain clarity on exactly what your dream looks like, so you can both visualize and verbalize it.

Now it is time to awaken your wildest dreams through motion, meditation, conversation, and rest, and in doing so, you will take the first step to make them a reality.

ACTIVITY 2.1: Awaken and Define the Dreams Your Heart Most Desires
TIME: 1 Hour
SUMMARY:

- Choose a peaceful place for your intentional dream experience.
- If you are feeling drowsy, take 6-12 minutes to nap before completing this exercise.
- Before drifting to sleep, or moving forward ask for clarity about a dream or experience you desire to attract into your life. For example, "Show me what good health looks and feels like," or "Show me what the next step is that I need to take to complete this project," or "Show me what my dream life looks like in the next three months."
- Reawaken your body with a few deep breaths (refer to activity 1.1), and a short walk outside. As you walk, be present with your steps and your thoughts. Let your mind wander into dreamland.
- When you return from your short walk, take the time to write down your life's grandest dreams and desires. Anything goes.
  - What have you always wanted to be, do, and have?
  - Where do you want to live? Do you own a vacation home?
  - What does your dream home look like? Fill in the details.
  - What does the relationship of your dreams look like? What do you do together? Do you have a family?
  - How does your healthy lifestyle look and feel? What do you eat?
  - Where do you want to explore?
- Once complete, review your work and highlight the words, statements, and sentences that make you feel most energized.
- Summarize why you want these dreams to become a reality.

- What will happen if you do not make your dreams a reality? What is the worst case scenario? Defining what will not happen if you do not work toward your dreams empowers you with a burning desire to make them come true.
- Lastly, share your dreams with a friend, family member, or trusted mentor.

CHAPTER 3

HEALTH TUNE-UP

"The key to a happy life is living an active, balanced, and healthy life-style that nourishes the mind, body, and spirit."

HEALTH IS OUR GREATEST WEALTH

Tapping into the power of a healthy lifestyle requires a personal commitment, plan, and daily discipline.

A wholesome, balanced, and active lifestyle will fuel your internal fire to wake up each day and live it in alignment with the person you truly wish to be. It will provide you with the sustainable long-term advantage necessary to be the greatest you. One that feels in tune, energized, and vibrant on a daily basis. Your youthfulness will return, transformational healing will happen, and the bedrock from which your new life launches will become sound.

THE POSITIVE ENERGY MODEL

The positive energy model states that what we fuel our body with also feeds our happiness, health, and overall success.

Focus on building positive momentum in your life, and as a result, you will attract more of what you most desire and work harder to maintain what you have earned.

OUR THOUGHTS BECOME THINGS

Pause before speaking because thoughts become words that drive actions which, if repeated, become habits and our way of life.

Honestly ask yourself - is what I am thinking fueling my life?

Does my speech inspire me and the world?

Do my actions align with my goals?

THE PEACEFUL MIND

Peace of mind should not be a hard road to travel to, because it is available right now in the present. With some conscious, consistent daily effort, you can retrain your brain to flow at ease through your daily tasks. It all starts with your thoughts. Fuel your mind with positive, self-assuring thoughts, and you will be on your way to living a peaceful, prosperous life.

But do not try to "think" your way to happiness. It will take work and the right nutritional balance.

POSITIVE VS. POISONOUS FUEL

Take a moment to drink some WATER.

NOT beer, soda, coffee, or any sugary garbage.

Plain, pure, water.

Taste the water, appreciate it, and think about it's source; a mountain stream, well, or spring. Smile at the glass of water you just got to drink.

WHY WATER?

Water fuels our mind, body, and spirit. It washes out toxins that accumulate each day and fuels our bodies' natural functions.

Pure water is just better than other liquids that we often consume.

Consumption of a gallon a day, depending on activity, will result in improved bodily function from head to toe.

Your body needs water to thrive. However, this just the beginning.

WE ARE WHAT WE EAT

A lot of what you might consume is poisoning your mind and body.

Alcohol, drugs, donuts, candy bars, sodas, and meats loaded with antibiotics hurt your bodies' ability to operate at a prime level of performance.

The most apparent habitual patterns are those that are also often overlooked. The impact of these habits accumulates over time, and have a compounded negative or positive effect on your health.

They can create a psychological and physical imbalance that results in injury, illness, and disease.

I realize this table is overly simplistic, but it provides a snapshot into what you may be putting into your body.

One fuels us; the other harms us.

NOURISHING (+)	HARMFUL (-)
<ul><li>Water</li><li>Organic Veggies</li><li>Organic Fruit</li><li>Organic Nuts</li><li>Organic Free-Range Eggs</li><li>Organic Antibiotic Free-Range Meat</li><li>Organic Dark Chocolate</li></ul>	<ul><li>Soda</li><li>Alcohol</li><li>Drugs</li><li>Donuts</li><li>Candy</li><li>Cake</li><li>Meat</li><li>Processed Rubble</li></ul>

Disclaimer: The table above gives examples of things you might consume. If you choose to consume better fuel, your body will naturally function better. Consulting a nutritionist before making any radical changes to your diet is suggested.

DIGITAL TECHNOLOGY OVERUSE

Technology has become a catalyst to massive change in the 21st century. Our widgets, gadgets, and thingamabobs are quite literally directing our way of life. I do not wish to bash on technology, but do believe our constant use of it can limit our views and restrict the natural human experiences that bring us happiness.

Experiences like a meal free of distractions, going on a walk in the woods without needing to document the entire journey, or just spending a day without your phone and computer.

I realize the need for technology in our world; it is a lifeline to building our businesses, supporting industry, and staying connected. It is, however, more important than ever to consciously look at your relationship with technology to improve your overall health.

TAKE A LOOK INTO YOUR CURRENT HEALTH

A health inventory is intended to inspire a conscious look at your current state of health. It is by no means comprehensive or designed to replace visits with healthcare professionals. After completing this exercise, pat yourself on the back for taking a significant step forward toward a healthier lifestyle.

ACTIVITY 3.1: Take Your Health Inventory
TIME: 30 Minutes
SUMMARY:

- Take the time to complete the included health inventory charts either within the book or in your notebook.
- Schedule appointments with your primary care doctor, nutritionist, physical therapist, athletic trainer, and any other necessary professionals.
- Most importantly, take action based on what you learn.

BODY	CURRENT	DESIRED	WHY/NOTES
Resting Heart Rate			
Blood Pressure			
Weight (lbs. or kg.)			
Vision			
Pain / Injuries			
Cosmetics			
Daily Exercise			
Illness			

FUEL	CURRENT	DESIRED	WHY/NOTES
Water Per Day			
Other Liquids (soda, alcohol, etc.)			
Veggies Per Day			
Fruit Per Day			
Protein Source			
Desserts			
Sleep / Night (hours)			

TECHNOLOGY (daily useage)	CURRENT	DESIRED	WHY/NOTES
Phone			
Computer			
TV			
Other			

HYGIENE	CURRENT (DAILY)	DESIRED (DAILY)	WHY/NOTES
Showers			
Wash Hands			
Brush Teeth			
Clean / Organize Living Space			
Clean Laundry (weekly)			
Clean Sheets (weekly)			
Clean Car (weekly)			

ENVIRONMENTAL IMPACT ON PERSONAL HEALTH

To live a healthier life, you must look at your environments: where you work, live, and play.

The places you spend most of your time has a more substantial impact on your health than you might imagine.

They have the power to lift you to higher heights or drag you down to lower lows.

ACTIVITY 3.2: Environmental Assessment
TIME: 10 Minutes
SUMMARY:

- Take a few minutes to complete the questions below. Be honest with yourself.
- What are the top three places where you spend most of your time?

USED TO BE: 1. _____ 2. _____ 3._____

NOW: 1. _____ 2. _____ 3._____

DESIRE TO BE: 1. _____ 2. _____ 3._____

- How do these places make you feel?
- Do they fuel you or drain you?
- Are you excited to spend time there, or would you rather be somewhere else?

OUR CIRCLE OF INFLUENCE

The people you choose to spend time around have a profound impact on what you end up doing with your career, free time, and life as a whole. They fuel your overall well-being, and you become a mirror reflection of these individuals.

If you genuinely want to change pieces of your life or your whole life, then assessing the people you surround yourself with is critical.

ACTIVITY 3.3: Circle of Influence Assessment
TIME: 10 Minutes
SUMMARY:

- Who are the top five people you spend the most time around?
- Do these people energize or drain you?
- Do their lives inspire you to be the person you want to be?
- Write these 5 people down.
  1. _____
  2. _____
  3. _____
  4. _____
  5. _____
- Consider changing the people you spend time around if they do not lift you up and fuel your desired life.

A SERIES OF HABITS BUILDS GREAT HEALTH

To build a healthy, balanced life, we must be willing to look at the habits that have become the foundation for getting us to here and now, since life is a direct result of what we repeatedly do.

Who you are today is a result of something you did in your past, and only you have the power to change that in the present as you flow into the future.

Take a moment to sit with this simple, yet powerful question:

Are my daily habits serving the life I truly wish to be living?

Some examples of habits to take an honest look at might include: getting consistent healthy sleep, not drinking alcohol or drinking less, exercising daily, stopping smoking, eating healthy food, and practicing a vegetarian lifestyle.

Use the framework on the next page to define the habits you wish to let go of and those you want to develop. By letting go of the bad things in your life, you open up more space for good experiences to happen. Your mind slowly becomes reprogrammed and better aligned with your dreams, visions, and goals.

One of the most significant steps toward living the life you have always imagined is changing habits that do not serve your success.

Take a moment to breathe and smile, because regardless of where you are, life is getting richer through this process of identifying healthy changes.

ACTIVITY 3.4: Define Your Healthy Habits
TIME: 30 Minutes
SUMMARY:

- Write your positive lifestyle changes in your notebook using the format below. Read your changes in the morning and at night. Remember, we become what we repeatedly do.
- Make a list of the habits you wish to change and what you will replace them with.
- Summarize your positive lifestyle change in 1-2 sentences.
- Consider the following questions when writing your new habits:
  - Why do I want to make this change, or why will my life become better?
  - What will happen if I do not make this change?
  - How am I going to make this change?
  - Who am I going to invite into my support network to support my healthy habits?
  - What daily actions can I take to make this a reality?

DAILY ACTIONS TO MAKE YOUR HEALTHY LIFE-STYLE A REALITY

- **Check in on a daily basis** to reflect on how you are feeling, what has been hard, and what you have learned. This conscious check only takes a moment.
- **Consistency:** Focusing on your positive changes daily basis will help you program them into your natural rhythm.
- **Create a Supportive Environment:** Your environment has a considerable influence on daily routines, your personality, and your wellbeing. Make sure that you adjust your environment to support your positive changes. You may even ask a friend or family member to either join your journey or, at the very least, support it.
- **Share Progress:** Keep your friends and family updated on your progress. Sharing your progress will inspire you to keep at it and maybe even help someone else.
- **Have Fun:** Most importantly, find the fun in these changes. Smile more, share the change, and enjoy the moment. Look for what you are learning from this experience and how it may shape a new lifestyle that is happier, healthier, and more positive.

COMMIT TO A HEALTHY LIFESTYLE

Honor yourself and the one life you get to live.

Fuel your dreams with excellent health.

In your notebook, write your commitment to a healthy lifestyle.

Here is mine:

I, Scott Rowley, under this massive old tree at Smith Rock State Park, Oregon, USA, commit myself to a clean, wholesome, balanced, active lifestyle that fuels the life of my dreams.

MEASURING YOUR PROGRESS

Building goals centered around your health empowers and energize you. They help keep you moving in the right direction to support the daily habits that you desire to bring into your life.

Goals are the implementation of a commitment to living a healthier lifestyle.

ACTIVITY 3.5: Set a Health Goal
TIME: 10 Minutes
SUMMARY:

- Cleary define a single health goal in your notebook. Focus the target on an event, injury, pain, dietary change, or really anything that helps move your life in a positive direction.
- It is _____ (date), _____ (time). I have successfully _____ (the goal you will accomplish), and as a result, I feel _____(how the accomplishment will make you feel).

Here is an example of a goal that I set and accomplished for myself:

It is December 31, 2017, at 24:00. I now weigh 175 lbs., which makes me feel vibrant, youthful, and energized. This goal is the result of living a healthy lifestyle. As a result of this healthy change, I feel alive and appreciative of who I am.

FUELING THE HUMAN SPIRIT

Our spirit, the non-physical part of our body, is fueled or extinguished by everything we do, every little thing. Each breath, snack, movement. It all contributes to our spirits' ability to thrive. To move our lives forward, backward or keep them static.

We have within us the ability to fuel our body to help push our lives in the direction we desire. Sadly, we also have the power to harm these forces.

There is energy in everything we choose to let into our lives and what we choose to filter out. It includes our thoughts, ideas, words, projects we work on, the food we consume, liquids we ingest, people we interact with, events we attend and everything that flows in and out of our entire body. We, not anyone else, decide what we say yes to and what we say no to by using our decision filters.

Fuel for your spirit can and should come from the sources that you most desire. You might find them in work, sports, community, food, literature, prayer, and meditation. Soon, you might discover that healthy fuel for your spirit is everywhere.

FUEL YOUR SPIRIT WITH BALANCE

A balanced life is peaceful, happy, and abundant. Strive for balance in all that you do, and happiness will be a constant presence.

How much of one thing and not another is enough to fuel your balanced lifestyle?

Taking a moment to step back and look at your whole life, the roles you play, and the time you spend in each can be incredibly powerful.

How much time do you spend at work, on personal adventures, active in the community, with family and friends, on financial planning, and in your home environment? All of these can fuel your human spirit.

What is missing that, if filled, would make your life feel full again?

Find your balance, keep it in tune, and embrace the fact that it will be ever changing.

ACTIVITY 3.6: Assess Your Life Balance
TIME: 30 Minutes
SUMMARY:

- The examples below represent components that create a happy fulfilling life. The point here is to focus on the areas of life that represent who you are and what matters to you.
- In your notebook rate yourself from 0-5 with a grade that represents how much energy you are investing in each area of life that matters. 0 being none at all and 5 being as much as I possibly can.
- Next write down a single, simple action item to make a change positive change in each area of your life.
- Areas of Attention:
  - Environment: Where you work, live, and play.
  - Money: How much $ you have, relationship with it, and what you spend it on.
  - Career: Your work and time spent on professional growth.
  - Relationships: Your friends, family, and people in your life.
  - Human Growth: What you do to grow personally.
  - Community: The town you live, your friends online, your tribe.
  - Spirituality: Your connection with your higher self.
  - Physical Health: Weight, energy, exercise, diet, etc.

MOTION MATTERS

Take a moment right now, before reading on, to get up wherever you are and move.

Do some push-ups, jumping jacks, or even stand up and stretch for a moment.

As one of my friends says, motion is the lotion.

He has built an active lifestyle and, as a result, can still do backflips on his skis at the ripe age of 50.

You see, motion matters more than we think. Our bodies are not designed to be sedentary 90% of the day, but many parts of the world have cultures that support this. Many of us sleep 8-9 hours, work sitting in a chair for 8-9 hours, travel from place to place sitting for 2-3 hours, eat for 2-3 hours, and we then have very little time for motion.

With so much sedentary time naturally built into our lives, we need to create time for movement. Build in physical activity. Make it a priority. Start your day with some form of exercise before jumping into the grind. Not just some days, weekends, or 3 days a week. Every day. Keep it simple: a morning walk, some light stretching, push-ups, jumping jacks. Just get the blood flowing. If this means you need to get up 15 minutes earlier, then do it. Your entire life will thank you.

ACTIVITY 3.7: Make Motion Part of Your Morning Routine
TIME: 15-30 Minutes Per Day
SUMMARY:

- Schedule in 15-30 minutes for motion as part of your morning routine.
- Keep the activity simple: a walk, a short yoga practice, or something active that brings you joy.

BUILD ON YOUR MORNING MOMENTUM

Morning activity is intended to set your day in motion, to allow your body some movement so it may naturally wake up, and to inspire the ripple effect of an active lifestyle. Additionally, this short time will help improve your brain's mental functioning right out of the gate.

As a result of tuning your body first thing, you will begin to look at your day from a little bit of a different angle. Opportunities for activity will start showing up, and taking advantage of them will seem like the natural thing to do. A group walk, run, hike, or daily trip the gym might become part of your active lifestyle.

Most importantly, find something you enjoy. If you do not like running because it hurts, then look for other options to keep your body in motion. I cannot emphasize the enjoyment factor enough because, if you do not enjoy it, then you will not continue doing it for very long.

MY ACTIVE LIFESTYLE

Here is a short list of activities I have built into my life to create an active lifestyle that keeps me mentally, physically, and spiritually strong. You will notice that I do not do any one thing. Instead, I do many things that help keep the spice of life alive for me. The activities I do also flex with the seasons, and my physical health, so I get to experience a variety in my lifestyle as the seasons and my body goes through change. Yoga is the only thing I practice on a daily basis; it is part of my morning routine that sets each day into a good flow for me.

- Yoga
- Skateboarding
- Ski (Mountaineering, Resorts, and Backcountry)
- Snowmobiling
- Rock Climbing
- Trail Running
- Hiking

- Backpacking
- Biking
- Adventure Motorcycling
- Working at My Stand-up Desk

Many of these activities are part of one adventure. For example, I might ride my adventure motorcycle to the base of a mountain, set up camp, go on a short run, then wake up the next day, flow through some yoga, and then go ski-mountaineering.

The point is that this is a lifestyle and not just a routine trip to the gym.

CONNECTING IT ALL: YOUR MIND, BODY, AND SPIRIT

Holistic health is at the core of our minds' ability to properly function, to lead our bodies' daily actions in the direction of our dreams. We indeed are what we choose to consume and do. Our mind, body, and spirit need good energy to burn a clean fire inside that fuels the life of our dreams.

As a result fueling our mind and body with great nourishment, we connect the two to a higher power that becomes an internal compass guiding our thoughts, actions, and overall being.

ACTIVITY 3.8: Inspire Your Healthy Lifestyle

TIME: Give yourself a 45-minute break to fuel your mind, body, and spirit.

SUMMARY:

- Mind: Complete 5 minutes of box breathing (refer to chapter 1).
- Body: Nourish your body for the next 30 minutes with motion, fuel, and hygiene.
- Motion: 15 minutes of walking, biking, running, yoga, or whatever it is that you enjoy.
- Fuel: 10 minutes to eat something small and healthy.
- Clean-up: 5 minutes.
- Spirit: Fuel your spirit for 10 minutes.
    - Prayer: A simple request, such as "Please bring peace, happiness, and prosperity to the world I am a part of."
    - Meditation: Sit with your prayer a minute.
    - Read: Choose something that is uplifting in a magazine, book, or listen to some music.
    - Nap: 5 minutes
- Journal Entry:
    - Before the activity: How do you feel? What are you thinking?
    - After the activity: How do you feel?

Always keep in mind that the greatest wealth is holistic health. And this is impacted by all areas of our lives. If we put too much emphasis on one area, then our healthy lifestyle is sure to suffer, and long-term side effects may begin to develop.

Use the positive, healthy lifestyle you are starting to build as your foundation for setting goals that matter to you, building a map to accomplish them, and pointing your energy in the right direction to make them a reality.

PART TWO:

CREATE A CLEAR MAP & FIND YOUR COMPASS

CHAPTER 4

SET GOALS & CREATE
A VISION THAT MATTERS

"Life changes when our 'someday' list becomes our 'NOW' list."

AVOID TARGET TUNNEL VISION

Goal-and results-oriented individuals often struggle with target tunnel vision. Meaning that after setting a goal, too often during the journey, we forget that each step of the process should be enjoyed. For, after all, why would we ever strive to achieve a goal that does not add more richness to life?

Somewhere along the path, we forget that each step is a gift and that the destination is in itself only a small fraction of the entire journey.

Not overdoing things, focusing for set amounts of time, and unplugging when our minds need a fresh perspective can help keep the joy alive in our endeavors.

While at times the journey can get hard, so long as a goal is right for us, meaning that it truly matters, then the route will be fun and energizing, ultimately making us richer physically, mentally, and spiritually.

ON GOALS

Desiring new objectives is natural. They help give us purpose in life and work. Goals help paint a pathway for us to improve our lives and make the world a better place.

Goals do not always have to mean more. Sometimes, they mean less. Like clearing our lives of things that longer serve us or losing a few pounds that are just extra baggage.

But sometimes, goals do mean more. Like maybe more money, a larger plot of land, or more books to read. These are not bad things, as long as they are used to improve life and add to its richness.

Goals help set a path to get us from where we are to where we want to be. If set correctly, they will naturally flow for us because they will be the right goals for our lives. Not set by an employer, school curriculum, institution or other person barking down our neck, telling us what we need to do with our lives. No, they'll be set by us, for us.

So, jump right in and set some goals that matter to you.

MINDSET MATTERS

Establish belief in yourself, define your goals, define a plan, clearly create a vision, take massive action and you will realize that you are capable of far more than you had ever thought possible, but you must first believe.

Start by believing in yourself and your untapped potential.

Taking a moment to establish a positive belief mindset will enhance your overall mood and help you believe that what once seemed impossible could become a reality.

ACTIVITY 4.1: Establish Belief
TIME: 3:00 Minutes
SUMMARY:

- Close your eyes for a few short minutes and visualize yourself living the life of your dreams. Or, if you already have a dream board, spend this time soaking in your vision. Paint vivid pictures in your mind.
- Believe the life you have envisioned is one you deserve and that nothing is impossible.
- Complete the sentence below.
- I believe I can (do, be, experience, or have) _____ because in the past I have proven to myself it is possible to (do, be, experience, or have)_____.

CLEARLY DEFINE GOALS THAT MATTER TO YOU

Your goals must matter to you. When you read them, they should ignite your spirit so you cannot wait for a new day to begin.

You may want to build a healthier lifestyle, travel the world, start a business, improve your relationships, go back to school, get a new job, or live happily in alignment with your purpose. To wake up each day inspired to do your work because you know in your heart that it matters.

Whatever your heart most desires, it must be clearly defined so you can see the pathway to the end in your sights. After all, if you don't know where you want to go, then how are you going to get there?

CORE LIFE AREAS FOR GOALS

Again, here are the areas in my life that I set goals for to keep living in balance.

I aim to always have a goal in each area to help keep my life fueled, balanced, and in tune with the person, I truly desire to be.

- Environment: Where you work, live, and play.

- Money: How much $ you have, relationship with it, and what you spend it on.
- Career: Your work and time spent on professional growth.
- Relationships: Your friends, family, and people in your life.
- Human Growth: What you do to grow personally.
- Community: The town you live, your friends online, your tribe.
- Spirituality: Your connection with your higher self.
- Physical Health: Weight, energy, exercise, diet, etc.

NOTE: Do not feel constrained by these core areas. Make them fit "you." If you do not have 60-90 minutes to complete the entire exercise now, start with one goal and come back to write goals for the other areas later.

ACTIVITY 4.2: Define your Goals and Create Your Vision Cards
TIME: 60-90 Minutes
SUMMARY:

- Use the following example to define your goals and create vision cards.
- You might also add your goals to a goals journal that you carry with you throughout your travels.
- On the front of the card, clearly define your goal.
- On the back create a vision card: a collection of images and words that will inspire you to continue taking action daily to make your goal a reality.
- Build your goal cards on a thick matte paper, or on large note cards.
- Read the cards twice a day to keep your goals in the front of your mind.

Here is an example of a goal/vision card that I created for myself.

Front:

Core Area of My Life: Health

Goal: It is December 31, 2017 at 24:00. I now weigh 175 lbs. as a result of living a healthier lifestyle.

Why I Want To Accomplish This Goal: This accomplishment makes me feel alive, strong, and appreciative of who I am.

If I Do Not Achieve This Goal: I will not be living life in alignment with my core values, radiating hope and prosperity to others all over the world.

How I Am Going to Accomplish This Goal: I will get to live this life by practicing yoga on a daily basis, eating healthier, and integrating more fun physical activity into my schedule.

Who Can Help Me: My Support Team

1. Ruth: Coach and Accountability Partner
2. Jarren: Mentor and Friend
3. Nate: Mentor, Friend, and Business Partner

Daily Actions:

1. Plan Activity into Each Day
2. Design Goals Around Active Living
3. Just Wake Up and Do It

1 Thing I Can Do Now:

- 12 Pushups

Reference: https://www.peakprosper.com/a-vision-for-healthy-living

Core Area of My Life:

_____

Goal:

_____

_____

Why I Want to Accomplish This Goal:

_____

_____

_____

If I Do Not Achieve This:

_____

_____

_____

How I Am Going to Accomplish This Goal:

_____

_____

_____

Who Can Help Me:

1. _____

2. _____

3. _____

Daily Actions:

1. _____

2. _____

3. _____

1 Thing I Can Do Now:

_____

_____

_____

BREAK EACH GOAL DOWN

"Mt. Everest has never been climbed in one day. It takes baby steps."

Like climbing Mt. Everest, a long-term goal can be a daunting objective. However, broken into a series of small steps taken one after the other, the daunting objective turns into a much more attainable target. By putting one step in front of the other, you will eventually reach the top.

Every long-term goal is reached by accomplishing a series of milestones and tasks. Break down your goal, make a plan, and begin taking action.

Take each of your goals that matter to you and break them down into 3-5 phases or milestones. Then define 3-5 steps that will help you accomplish each milestone. You may need more steps to achieve your goal; the key is to break it down into digestible and realistic chunks so you can start making progress.

In your notebook, write out your goals, their phases, each step to complete each stage, and someone that can help you accomplish them. Write as much detail as you need to break down your goals into realistic tasks. Breaking your large goals down will make taking action much more manageable than otherwise.

Here is a framework you can use to outline the milestones and tasks for each of your goals.

YOUR GOAL:

- PERSON TO HELP ME:
  - PHASE I:
    - STEP 1:
    - STEP 2:
    - STEP 3:
  - PHASE II:
    - STEP 1:
    - STEP 2:
    - STEP 3:
  - PHASE III:
    - STEP 1:
    - STEP 2:
    - STEP 3:

GET THEM ON A REAL CALENDAR

We all have a limited amount of time each year.

While many of us wish we had superpowers that enabled us to do everything we imagined, that is not possible. Without scheduling what we are going to do, it is easy to end up planning too much or wasting time doing things that do not matter. Saying yes to too many things leads to feeling overwhelmed and making little to no progress on our goals.

Next, take some time to schedule out your year by clearly blocking out when you will focus on what. Also, be respectful of your life. For example, if you have plans to launch a new brand in January, then traveling for the entire month is probably not congruent with this. If some of your goals will require a full year, then write down your phases and steps on the months and days you will take action.

ACTIVITY 4.3: Get a Calendar and Schedule Your Goals
TIME: 30 Minutes
SUMMARY:

- Get a new calendar and schedule your goals by month. Not a digital calendar, but a real calendar that you will look at throughout each day.
- You may also consider scheduling your goals into your digital calendar, but do not overlook the magic of having a tangible timeline of your goals.

DEFINE YOUR DOMINO

A domino goal activates the cumulative effect produced when one event sets off a chain of similar incidents.

What is your domino goal?

What is the one goal on your list that, when accomplished, will empower you with the energy and resources to make all of your other goals attainable?

Maybe you have multiple perceived domino goals, but there is likely one that will have the most significant impact on completely transforming your life.

Write your domino goal on the back of a few notecards and place it in your wallet, on your nightstand, in your car. Read it whenever you have an extra minute. Program your subconscious to work on this goal even when you are working on something else.

BUILD A CLEAR VISION TO ACTIVATE THE LAW OF ATTRACTION

You can begin today by attracting the life you have always dreamed of with the power of a vision board. Also known as a dream board, this tool will help you create more clarity around who you are, want to be, and what your goals will look like once they are a reality.

Vision boards are a visual representation of your goals, desires, and life you wish to live. Your board will be comprised of images, pictures, words, quotes, affirmations, and goals that provide you with a snapshot into your future.

The following key elements create a powerful vision board:

- **Visuals:** Images, pictures, and symbols that align with your goals and the ideal vision you have for life.
- **Power Words:** These might change over time, but they carry with them the true meaning about who you are at the core. They might be your values or words that inspire you. Example words: Health, Love, Happiness, Prosperity, Inspiring, Community, Adventure, Travel
- **Quotes:** Your favorite quotes or sayings that encourage you to be the best and most energized you.
- **Affirmations:** A statement framed as already being your current reality, regardless of your present circumstances. For example "I am worthy of my dreams." "I am vibrantly healthy and thriving inside my beautiful body."

To begin, find pictures that symbolize the experiences, things, and feelings you want to attract into your life. You will see these in photographs, magazines, pamphlets or online. Begin cutting them out or printing them. Organize your words and images neatly on a board that is big enough to fit your needs, 3 feet by 2 feet is about right.

Once your board is complete, put it in a place that you can view it in the morning upon awakening and at night before you fall asleep. If you built a vision board for your business, then consider placing it in your office where you can look at it throughout the day and use it as a source of inspiration to keep you going.

Here is some additional suggested reading with a summary of the supplies you will need, stories of others having used vision boards, visualization exercises and examples to inspire the creation of yours: peakprosper.com/the-power-of-a-vision-board

ACTIVITY 4.4: Build Your Vision Board
TIME: 1-2 Hours
SUMMARY:

- Schedule some uninterrupted time to complete your board.
- Collect your vision board supplies.
- Build your board.
- Share your board with friends, family, and in your online network.

BRINGING IT ALL BACK TOGETHER

If you are to this point and have not completed the suggested activities, then please go back and put some time into defining what you want to accomplish. Because, after all, it is impossible to get somewhere when we do not know where that somewhere is.

Through this last chapter, you did a lot of work. So, take a moment to congratulate yourself, pause for a breath, and prepare for the fun part. The work.

At this moment, remind yourself that failing to accomplish one's goals is often the result of quitting or not starting, and remember, you are not a quitter.

At this point, you now clearly know where you want to go, and you have a plan to get there. It is time to start taking action and find joy in the journey to your next destination.

Embrace the fact that some days will be hard, but in the end, it will all be worth it.

Here we go. Forward.

CHAPTER 5

THE JOYFUL JOURNEY

"Set a goal, make a plan, and flow into the joy of each step on your journey, for then you will have found an ultimate form of success."

FINDING THE BALANCE POINT

There is joy to be experienced during each step of the journey toward a destination in life. This does not mean work will be free from challenges and upset, rather that we get a choice to appreciate the process, let go of the demand for a specific result and dance through the fun of each task, human interaction, question, training session, and progress on our joyful journey toward realizing the life of our dreams.

I believe joy is a point of balance found between discipline and spontaneous living where we experience a state of flow. Never be so spontaneous that life lacks discipline, for freedom will be a blur and chaos will ensue. Our goals will fall by the wayside, and constant disruption will become the norm. Find a balance between the two, and you are sure to find the joyous and free life you were always after.

COMMITMENT - A KEY INGREDIENT

Self-discipline is a personal commitment to yourself.

It's a commitment that you will do what it takes, no matter what, to accomplish what your heart most desires.

Because if you genuinely want to realize your dreams, accomplish your goals, and experience personal freedom, then discipline and hard work are critical.

DISCIPLINE IS...

Focusing on the tasks that matter.

Ridding your environment of distractions.

Working hard every day, not just some days.

Playing hard every day so your work is fun.

Living life for yourself and for those who have passed before you.

Fueling your mind, body, and spirit with a healthy, balanced, and active lifestyle.

Sometimes skipping the party because you have work to do.

Waking up early because, after all, the early bird always gets the worm.

Doing what is needs done even when you would rather be somewhere else.

Count on your self-discipline because you are the only person who can put in the work and the long days. You are the only person who can continue to step towards the starting line and run the race even after it feels like defeat has just washed over you.

Discipline is defining what you do with your time each day, week, month, and year. Because, after all, if you do not specify this, then someone else will define it for you.

DAILY DISCIPLINE

Consciously looking at your environment, the people you choose to surround yourself with, and how well you stick to your plan for each day will empower you with the ability to add more ease to your life.

"Own your day, and you'll own your life."

Creating a 24-hour routine that supports your goals and following it will fuel all aspects of life that truly matter. You will become the master of your domain, and no matter what you will win.

Remember, 24 hours is not a lot of time.

When we break our day down and look at how our time is used, we gain the power to identify areas of opportunity to focus on our goals that matter.

Your 24-hour day likely looks much different than mine, and it should. Perhaps you sleep longer or spend less time training for things. Maybe you have a full-time job that requires you to be at the office during a set period each day. Write all of these blocks into your schedule. This exercise's primary benefit is to help you identify pockets of time that can be utilized to work on your goals, self-care, and overall wellbeing.

Creating your 24-hour schedule requires that you identify how your time is spent. Write out when you do what each day, and fill in your framework. Use my schedule to inspire yours. Most importantly, you should identify when you spend time on the following key things:

- Self-care: Health, Fitness, Hygiene, Eating, etc.
- Work: Goals associated with a new career and time at your current job.
- Sleep: Schedule at least 8 hours per night.
- Free Time: Enjoy life, do what sings to you.
- Naps: Give yourself some time throughout the day to rest and recharge.

The next page has a snapshot of my 24-hour day. Since my day might be overwhelming, let me preface it with a confession. I do not follow this schedule to a T, but it gives me a framework to support the goals that matter most to me. And yes, I do strive to get my butt out of bed every day at 04:30 even when I am tired because this time is sacred to me. It's free of interruptions because everyone else is usually sleeping, and it gives me two hours of self-care that help set my day into flow rather than just jumping straight into work.

You will see that I divide my day into two to three hour time blocks. During these blocks, I take time to listen to what my body needs, eat when I am hungry, sleep when I am tired, and move when I need a little motion. While I strive to honor this time each day of the week, I do give myself permission to unplug from my routine and welcome the serendipity of life to thrive.

And finally, most importantly, I have elected to write my domino goal and purpose at the top of my 24-hour schedule, so I read it multiple times per day.

Scott's 24-Hour Day

#1 Goal: To regain full foot strength and mobility enabling me to go trekking in Nepal from October 1, 2019 - October 30, 2019.

My purpose is to use my adventurous spirit and passion for personal excellence to inspire and empower people, communities, and businesses around the world.

- 04:30-06:30 | **Fuel Your Spirit**: Rise & Shine – Honor the New Day
- Make Your Bed, Drink Water, Coffee, & Tea, Prayer, Foot Care, Yoga (sweat), Meditation, Reading, Gratitude Journal, Read Goals, Review Plan for the Day
- **Fuel Your Health:** Eat Some Good Nutritious Food
- **Hygiene & Self-care:** Shower, Short Nap, and Get Settled
- 06:30-09:30 | **Work on #1 Goal:** Make Progress Every Day
- 10:00-12:00 | **Fuel Your Work:** Event Planning, Digital Course & Content Development, Coaching & Consulting, Product Development, Strategic Planning
- 12-12:15 | **Power Nap**
- 12:15-13:00 | Lunch & Rest
- 13:00-16:00 | **Fuel Your Work & Your Athlete**
- 16:00-17:00 | **FREEDOM** to do as I please.
- 17:00-19:00 | Athletic Training, Spiritual Time, Yoga, etc.
- 19:00-20:00 | Disconnect for Dinner
- 20:00-21:00 | Hygiene, Foot Care, Read, and Reflect
- 21:00 – 04:30 | SLEEP | Recover

ACTIVITY 5.1: Define Your Own 24-Hour Schedule
TIME: 30-minutes
SUMMARY:

- Refer to Scott's 24-Hour Schedule for inspiration.
- Your Schedule Should Include:
  - Your #1 Goal and Purpose Statement
  - Blocks of Time to Complete Key Things Throughout Your Day: Self-care, work, sleep, free time, and naps.
- Type your 24-hour schedule into a digital document and print it, or write it on a piece of paper.
- The main purpose of this activity is to identify time to focus on what is most important to you.

POWER ROUTINES FOR CREATING GREATNESS

Consistency will make you a winner.

It will empower you with the ability to create greatness in all areas of your life.

Like baking a great batch of healthy energy bars, getting the formula right will take some time, and there is always room for improvement.

These daily, weekly, monthly, and annual rituals will help set your life on a path that you pave. Keep it simple, follow a structure, and make it your own.

Here is a snapshot of the routines that I go through on a daily, weekly, monthly, and annual basis. These help me maintain momentum in life and business.

Daily Rituals:

1. Plan your day. And visualize your future.
2. Review your goals, in order to keep them at the forefront of your mind.
3. Gratitude. Take the time to write down three things you are grateful for on a daily basis.

Gratitude attracts more of what you most desire out of life.

Weekly Rituals:
1. Plan your week.
2. Clean your space (office, home, car, laundry, etc.).
3. Review the big picture. Where do you want to be in 5 years?

Monthly Rituals:
1. Plan priorities for the month.
2. Review progress / achievements from last month.
3. Schedule time for fun.

Annual Rituals:
1. Review your past year.
2. Celebrate accomplishments and failures.
3. Create an inspiring plan for the next year.

ACTIVITY 5.2: Define Your Routines and Rituals
TIME: 30-minutes
SUMMARY:

- Clearly define 2-3 daily, weekly, monthly, and annual routines to put some structure into your life.
- Schedule these routines into your life so they become habit.

Supporting Material: Peak Prosper Guide to Setting Goals That Matter. Download for free at peakprosper.com/resources.

TAKE ACTION EVERY DAY

Most importantly, continue taking action every day in ways that support your goals and your ideal future life.

And, when the going gets tough, as it will, call one of your friends, or mentors for a dose of motivation to keep moving forward.

Some days, taking action might just be writing in your journal that you needed a self-care day to unplug from your goal and reflect on your progress. Other days, taking action might mean a 12-hour push.

While plans are critical to point us in the right direction, things never go exactly as we plan. By embracing this fact, we open our minds up to what brings life balance and joy.

NO LONGER FUN

While it is a cliché fact, life is short, and we only get to live it once.

If a goal, career, or passion project is no longer fun, then start seriously asking why.

Why am I still doing this? Has the fun factor completely gone away, or am I just a bit burned out?

Be honest in your response to these questions, and honor the change that might be necessary for you to move back into a state of joyful living.

NEW ADVENTURES

Your human desire to experience new adventures, grab coffee with a friend who is in town or do something that breaks up your routine will always come calling just when life seems to be drying up, or even when life is already full.

New adventures fuel so many aspects of our lives. They inject creativity into problem-solving, inspire new solutions to everyday life, and help pave the pathway for new relationships, goals, and ways of living.

As long as we remain willing and open to new experiences that may arise in a moment's notice, then life will be full. It will be rich with laughter and good times.

Just as discipline is necessary for success and happiness, equally so are spontaneous adventures.

OPEN MINDEDNESS

Keeping an open mind for these spontaneous moments to occur every day will help free you from the stereotypical box of living and working within a constrained environment and routine.

This mindset opens us up to new ideas and opportunities that we might not otherwise see. And it is easier to move into this state of mind than one might think. By shifting from a closed mindset focused on self to one that is open to other thoughts, ideas, and opinions, we begin to open up to a new world of possibility.

SOME IDEAS TO BREAK A ROUTINE

Here is a short list of things you might consider to break a routine from living, working, and playing in the same place.

- Download all necessary documents and work offline in the woods or a park for a day. (Yes, you can go hiking and work on the same adventure. You do not need the Internet.)
- Check out the local community boards in town for fun new events that are happening, then show up to one.
- Take a nap when you are tired.
- Spend extra time with friends and family even if you have something going on the next day since time with loved ones matters.
- Stay at a party a bit longer because you are having fun. Who knows what the next conversation might inspire?
- Break up a work session that has slowed down with some push-ups, a new work environment, a hike, a bike ride, a short walk outside, a conversation with a stranger, a magazine, or a fresh cup of coffee.

BE SPONTANEOUS. BE DISCIPLINED. FIND THE JOYFUL BALANCE.

Honor your human need for both discipline and spontaneity in your life, and you will experience the joyful journey to prosperity.

Throughout your journey toward accomplishing the goals that matter to you, come back to the following questions when life feels a little out of balance. They will help reignite your fire to keep pressing forward when the going gets tough or inspire a new direction.

Do I feel like my goal or goals are still serving me?

Which goal or goals are causing the most frustration in my life?

Why does this frustration exist?

What can I do about this goal to make the journey toward success fun again?

Is the sacrifice of discipline and work still worth continuing?

Can and should I set my goal aside for a short time to reboot, then return to it with new energy?

Do not underestimate the power of these questions, especially the last one. I have first-hand experience with setting some goals aside to work on other things for a few days. After returning with new energy, the process seemed to flow with more ease and excitement. There is something magical about bringing new energy to a project.

A PROJECT TO BRING LIFE MORE JOY

A joy project is one of these most powerful ways to create the necessary headspace and positive energy to move your goals and life to the next level.

This project requires you to take an honest look at what brings you happiness in life and what does not. If something does not bring you positive energy, then a change of some kind will be necessary.

The sum of this entire exercise will likely take more than 30-minutes, but setting aside this time to at least begin will most certainly empower you with the ability to start honestly looking at what brings happiness in your life and what does not.

ACTIVITY 5.3: Create Your Own Joy Project
TIME: 30-minutes
SUMMARY:

- Set aside a block of time to honestly look at your relationships, "things," behaviors, and goals. Ask yourself one question: Does this bring me joy?
- If something does not bring you joy, then make a plan to change it or get rid of it.

BRINGING US BACK INTO BALANCE

The balance of discipline and spontaneity will help you not lose the spice of life as you travel on the road to your accomplishments. Honoring the need for balance in everything you do, as well as not letting your drive for success lead you to isolation or a closed mind, will result in a more prosperous and joyful life.

Always remember, experiencing joy is an ultimate form of success.

CHAPTER 6

COMMUNITY CONNECTION AND CONTRIBUTION

"Give without expectation, and in return, you will receive more than you could have possibly imagined."

STRONGER WITH COMMUNITY

Connection to your community will make you stronger, happier, and more inspired.

It provides a strong sense of purpose to life.

With community, we build a sense of team which represents more than just a group of people. It makes everything matter.

Together Everything Accomplished Matters = TEAM

In contrast, something accomplished alone is just not as rewarding.

With a team, nearly everything is possible, we are stronger, our imaginations are more inspired, and an environment for all of us to stand up and lead is created, resulting in life-changing experiences. Without a team, most everything is more challenging, or in many cases impossible.

CONNECTING TO COMMUNITY

There are so many ways to connect to a community because it is quite literally everywhere.

It is in nature, yoga classes, social media, places of employment, local organizations, plane flights, train and bus rides, and commutes to work.

Connecting to your community will provide a stronger sense of meaning than most anything else in life.

However, making these connections, just like living the life of your dreams, is all on you.

You have to reach out, show up, and maintain the relationships.

Making connections can be simple. It does not have to become a daunting task.

It can be going on a hike outside, participating in a yoga class, or showing up to the next community service project.

Connecting with others does not have to take a significant amount of time, but doing it every day is essential. I call it a daily dose of community connection.

BUILDING STRONG RELATIONSHIPS

We all desire strong, healthy, and happy relationships that lift us up and provide support when it is needed.

Building these relationships takes a willingness to...

show-up and follow up
be all there
be present and unplugged
be kind
share your story
be a perfectly imperfect YOU

Do not expect your community to bloom overnight. It will take time, but always believe it will happen.

Show up when the next opportunity for adventure arises, explore something new that might be a little outside of your comfort zone, and when you are there, be present.

Unplug from your technology devices, so you can plug into what truly matters: Community Connection.

Your next opportunity to connect to your community has been waiting for someone like you for a long time. Someone inspiring, brave, daring, and bold who is willing to seek out the next opportunity to lead or be part of a group, service project, or conversation. To do something that has a positive impact on the world.

RECONNECT

To truly reconnect to our community, we must first disconnect from digital distractions and the confines of self. We must un-self.

Un-self: looking beyond our single unit of humanity to seek new opportunities to connect.

Go ahead, put your phone, watch, computer, and other digital devices away. You will be okay without them for the next five minutes.

RELAX.
BREATHE.
LET GO.

Disconnecting for a few minutes will strengthen your human connection to the natural world and other people around you.

It will free your mind from the digital slavery that is controlling our daily lives and open room for you to create and connect to the spiritual magic of community.

Take a moment right now to connect with your team, family, friends, or the great outdoors. You are about to discover that community is everywhere.

ACTIVITY 6.1: Make a Community Connection
TIME: Less than 5 minutes
SUMMARY:

- Disconnect from technology and the act of doing for just a moment and take the time to make a strong connection with your surrounding environment.
- Go on a short walk outside without your phone, enjoy a short conversation, or just sit in still observation for a few minutes disconnected from technology.

CONNECTED TO SOMETHING LARGER THAN SELF

Community connection will bring you much joy and fulfillment in life. New relationships will be formed, new paths will be traveled, and opportunities you never even knew were lurking around the next corner will start to show up every day.

If you felt alone in this world, that feeling will disappear. New energy will fuel your spirit on a daily basis.

Most importantly, you will be given a strong sense of purpose and meaning to life. If you already had this purpose, then consciously engaging with your community will take it to the next level.

Also, in making new connections, we receive unique opportunities to stand up and contribute to other causes, businesses, and things that bring our lives joy, and a strong sense of belonging.

CONTRIBUTING TO COMMUNITY

Every day, opportunities sit right in front of us to give back to the local community we each call home. They are everywhere we look, and all it takes is one little action to create a positive ripple effect in your life and someone else's. Little things await like picking up a single piece of trash, taking a moment to hold the door for someone at a coffee shop, or standing up against a bully because it is the right thing to do.

These micro givebacks can be fun. Like life, not all of them will be awesome, but through each experience in giving back, we will bring smiles to the faces of others, make new friends, and create positive trends by becoming better individuals ourselves.

Each day, strive to contribute more than you take. Giving more than your community gives you will mean that in times of trial and tribulation that inevitably come in life, a strong support network will be there for you. It is true that in helping others, we naturally help ourselves.

Like I said, your acts of contribution should be fun. Just like work and life, don't do them if you don't feel natural happiness in them. Find something that fuels your spirit. I've found that organizing community bonfires, service projects, picking up trash daily, and smiling at strangers are some of the top ways in which I can give back and find joy in doing so.

You may very well copy these or find some acts of goodwill that are entirely different. The important thing is to find something that inspires you to take consistent action, resulting in a healthier, happier community in which you live, work, and play.

WHAT'S IN IT FOR ME

When you begin giving on a routine basis without expecting anything in return, rewards will start to show up in the most serendipitous ways. They will become a byproduct of your contribution, and what you receive in return will inevitably have a compound effect, meaning that the delayed rewards of giving will far outweigh those of instant gratification (although you may experience that instant gratification as well).

The positive psychological effect of giving will hit you during or directly after a generous act. Also, if you continue to give on a daily basis, your health, happiness, and longevity will improve.

Anything you truly need to support your life will show up as a result of freely contributing to your community. Whether your needs are related to career, health, or another area of life, your community will be behind you to provide the necessary support for personal and professional growth.

Don't believe me? Give it a try yourself. Go reach out to your local support network.

The next activity is intended to become an ongoing source of inspiration until daily giving, and community connection becomes an integral part of your lifestyle. Remember that often, the smallest conscious acts help create a positive ripple effect.

Creating time in your schedule for local community service events is fun and rewarding, and it provides a tremendous sense of accomplishment. This does not need to take an entire day. Donating 1-2 hours of your time will be more than enough to have an incredible impact. In a few short hours, you might make some new friends while having an impact that results in other people helping out. You will most certainly feel as though the work you did mattered.

Take one of the ideas below and run with it. Do not overthink it. Why spend 30 minutes thinking, when you could already be 30 minutes into the beginning of your worthy cause?

I understand you may not have all the time in the world to give, which is why the ideas on the next page have been organized by time commitment.

Remember, you do not have to do something huge to have a positive impact. Just do something.

ACTIVITY 6.2: Acts of Community Contribution
TIME: a few hours – multiple days
SUMMARY:

- Pick one or several of the suggested activities below, then do it.
- Micro Moments to Minutes:
    - Pick Up Some Trash
    - Hold the Door for Someone
    - Smile at a Stranger
    - Give Someone a Hug
    - Share a Positive Social Media Comment on A Friend's Post
- Hours:
    - Go on a Community Hike
    - Volunteer a Few Hours at Your Library
    - Become a Mentor Once a Week
    - Publish a Blog Post that Benefits Your Community
    - Clean Up a Park
- Days:
    - Join a Service Project (Search Online for Your Town + Community Service Projects)
    - Build Your Own Project
        - Adopt a Park
        - Trash Cleanup
        - Build a Trail
    - Create a Food Donation Drive
    - Sponsor a Family During the Holidays

Now go out and connect to your community by making some small contribution. You will feel happier, healthier, and more inspired by your work and life as a result of taking this small action forward.

PART THREE:

Take Massive Action

CHAPTER 7

LIFE ON PURPOSE

Live your life on purpose, and you will feel energized like never before.

Defining and living your purpose will help fill your days with more excitement and provide a fulfilling reason for why you do your work.

DEFINING PURPOSE

What if you lack purpose or do not know where to find it?

SIMPLE.

Define your purpose. Your heart already knows what it is.

Keep it simple and do not overthink it.

ACTIVITY 7.1: Define Your Purpose
TIME: 5 – 30 minutes
SUMMARY:

- Begin by writing words that represent moments, experiences, and things in life that make you feel alive (everything goes).
- Use this question to help inspire your thoughts: What were the top three moments in the last 1-5 years in which you felt the most alive, happy, free, and lost in the moment?
- Highlight 5-10 of your words that bring you the most energy.
- Use 3-5 of those words to create your purpose statement.
- NOTE: Do not feel constrained to this process, or structured sentence template.
- Complete the purpose sentence below:
  - My purpose is to _____ (one of your passions, strengths, or power words) to ____ (how living this will improve the world).

Write your purpose in multiple places where you will read it throughout the day (notebook, 24-hour schedule, wallet card, vision board, etc.)

WORK HARD

Once your purpose is defined, then WORK HARD.

Use EVERY DAY to live your purpose because the world needs you.

At the same time, never forget that some days, working hard means resting.

Always strive to keep it simple.

And when things get hard, as they will, persevere because the result of your work will always be worth the reward.

Temporary pain will never hurt as bad as a permanent defeat. So when it hurts, pause. Rest. Give your body what it needs, but always keep your purpose in the front of your mind.

As a result of hard work, your goals, happiness, and the life you most desire will start to become what you experience as you flow through each day.

There is no denying the fact that your purpose and dreams are going to take A LOT of WORK.

This hard work will result in a stronger, faster, smarter, and happier version of you.

It will set you free and empower you with the internal fire that is critical to living the life of your dreams, to being fulfilled and full of what your heart most desires. On your journey, hard work will be a friend some days and an enemy on other days. At times, work will flow, but at other times, it will feel like you are swimming upstream.

During these times, stay disciplined and keep moving forward. Keep working your plan one step and one day at a time.

PLAY HARD

Joke, laugh, listen to music, and find joy in what you spend your time doing.

When you are stuck, frustrated, or confused, inject some joy into your work, but keep working hard. As long as the goals you are after are in alignment with your purpose, they will not feel like work. In fact, they will feel like play.

After all, we spend a large portion of life working, so why use it doing something we do not enjoy?

Whether you are a postman, cashier, corporate executive, entrepreneur, or indeed anyone, it is possible to enjoy the work you are doing with the right frame of mind.

Smiling, showing gratitude, and putting forth positive energy during each step of your journey will inspire your work and those who are part of it. Naturally, new opportunities will begin showing up.

However, some days, work will just not be fun. While we all likely wish we could love our work all the time, sometimes it is merely a means to making what we enjoy possible.

Instilling play into your daily life will almost certainly give you the spark to fire up your day early and make the most out of each moment.

LIVE LIFE

This is your ticket to show up to your life and live it to the fullest.

Begin experiencing joy in everyday jobs by appreciating your work in the present.

Believe in the person you are becoming; a human who at her or his core knows that living their dreams will bring them a life with a happy destiny.

So.

Get up before the birds.

Work toward living the life of your dreams.

Start making the changes that energize you.

Take a breath, feel the spark, and inspire your fire.

You will know when you are truly living life. Each day will feel full, rich, and abundant.

ACTIVITY 7.2: Inject Joy and Play into Your Daily Life
TIME: 5-10 Minutes
SUMMARY:

- Breathe.
- Drink some water.
- Do one or all of these simple actions to bring joy into your work:
    o Schedule a walk break outside.
    o Make time today to do something you love.
    o Give your coworker or person near you a high five or a hug.
    o Write a note of gratitude to someone.
    o Take a moment to laugh at the work you currently get to work on.
    o At least smile. ☺

PURPOSEFUL PROGRESS

By now, you are well on your way to a version of you that is happier, healthier, and more inspiring.

You are working toward or already found a natural rhythm to your days, replaced bad habits with good ones, and began taking massive action.

Don't quit, and do not get complacent.

Keep moving your life forward, closer to the life of your dreams filled with freedom, happiness, and service.

Now, take a moment to rewrite your domino goal from chapter 4 into your notebook. And honestly ask yourself the following questions:

- Have I been making progress on this goal daily?
- Am I now willing to commit to this goal 100%? To do everything necessary to win.

If your answer to the last question was no, then take a moment now to rethink your domino goal. Maybe it is the wrong goal for you, or perhaps now is not the time.

Or perhaps a shift and recommitment need to occur so you can accomplish your objective.

RETHINK. REWRITE. REWIRE.

If your domino goal is no longer something that fires you up, then take a moment to rethink it. Is it still the right goal for you? Does it support where you truly want to be?

Rewrite your goal, make some small or significant changes so that it does align with the life of your dreams. And most importantly, continue taking action on a daily basis to move your life closer to where your heart most desires.

ACTIVITY 7.3: Schedule 3 Uninterrupted Hours to Work on Your Domino Goal
TIME: 3 Hours
SUMMARY:

- Accomplishing your one domino goal that aligns with your purpose is going to take consistent, focused work. Take a moment to create three hours of time for you to focus on this goal.
- **WHEN** can you realistically dedicate this time? Can you make it an everyday thing? Can you shuffle your schedule or start waking up at 04:30 to make it happen?
- **WHERE** will you be able to find the focus and inspiration necessary to fuel consistent, productive action? Make a list of your top 3 places that are easy to reach and that support your work.
- **RESOURCES**: What resources do you need to fuel your goal and your purpose? What is missing? This could be things like money, friendships, and connections, or something else.

The fact will always remain that building a life on purpose is like nothing you will have ever experienced before. It will take work and transformational changes to what you do on a day-to-day.

Take a few moments today to re-read your purpose, share a smile with someone, enjoy a deep breath, and lend a helping hand to a stranger.

Most importantly, start living your purpose every single day.

CHAPTER 8

MAINTAIN MOMENTUM

"The more momentum we build, the more our lives keep moving forward."

WHAT DOES IT MEAN TO MAINTAIN MOMENTUM?

Maintaining momentum simply means to keep moving forward at the rate we have established.

Keep flowing, and progress will continue to happen as long as you have built a sustainable pace and continue moving forward every single day.

But embrace the fact that, at times, we may need to rest from movement to restore the energy necessary to keep moving forward.

In these times of rest, we can mentally maintain our momentum knowing that when the time comes again to make progress, our pace will already have been set, and routine will go back into motion.

DO NOT STOP BOTH MENTALLY AND PHYSICALLY

Keep moving forward.

Do not stop.

You got your life rolling in the right direction, and with each step forward, it grows.

You get faster, stronger, and smarter. Maintaining your momentum becomes more fluid.

The momentum of your life is building. Keep it in motion.

And when it slows, let it.

Let it slow because sometimes, that is just life catching up with you and your incredible imprint on the world.

Maintain your driving force, embrace the energy that you have flowing through you, and continue moving forward.

THE MOMENTUM MAINTENANCE METHOD

To maintain what we have built, we need to have a repeatable process to keep us moving in the right direction every day. The following three components are the factors required to continue advancing toward your objective.

MOMENTUM MAINTENANCE = Advancement + Support + Positive Affirmation

Advancement:

You are taking action every day.

No matter how small, you do something every day to advance.

Whatever you do, do not come to a complete standstill.

Each micro-action you take will add up, getting you to where you truly want to be.

If you take a day to stop, it will just be that much harder to pick up where you left off.

Whatever you do, keep moving forward.

Support:

Build your support network larger every day.

Reach out to others.

Share your progress.

You will get stronger, and others will help you build your momentum into an unstoppable force.

Affirmations:

Most importantly, fuel your mind with positive affirmations that you are building what you are meant to create.

Feed yourself positive self-talk...

I am enough. I am crushing it. I am making progress toward the dreams I always wanted to live. I am right where I need to be in this moment.

At the same time, ask others for feedback.

Sometimes it will be positive, and other times it will be critical feedback points that provide you with the necessary insight to get your sails pointed in the right direction.

This feedback might boost your energy or deflate you for a moment, but either way, it will become a power to fuel your momentum.

FUEL YOUR MOMENTUM

Always remember that life needs high-quality fuel.

Your spirit, mind, body, work, and community need positive energy every day.

They need good fuel for the fire.

Take a moment to look back at chapter 3, Health Tune-up, to reflect on the fuel you are giving your human engine.

Are you getting enough of the good stuff?

Water.

Veggies.

Positivity.

BOOST YOUR MOOD WITH POSITIVE PERSONAL PRAISE

Writing down daily actions that we are proud of helps us build momentum, and improve our mood by consciously looking back at the progress we have made toward our goals.

ACTIVITY 8.1: Give Yourself Some Praise

TIME: 30-60 Seconds

SUMMARY:

- Write down 1-3 things that you are proud of accomplishing from the last 24 - 48 hours.
- Breathe.
- Smile.

REFLECTING ON PROGRESS TO BUILD MORE MOMENTUM

Reflecting on your progress at the end of every day, or even throughout the day, will help fuel your unstoppable fighting spirit to continue pushing toward realizing the life of your dreams.

Consciously taking a moment to write down what did or did not get done is a critical factor for maintaining momentum.

I know we touched on this in goal setting, but I believe it needs to be reexamined again in a different light, as a reminder that each day we have 24 hours to sleep, eat, and experience life.

Planning how we spend each day helps us prioritize our lives and makes flowing into a new day a smooth transition. In many ways, it gives us freedom and allows us to see pockets of previously wasted time to work on what truly matters.

ACTIVITY 8.2: Evening Reflection and Planning
TIME: 5-15 Minutes
SUMMARY:

- PLAN: Your simple daily plan should answer four questions:
    - How will I spend my time?
    - What are my goals for this day? (Focus on 1-3 goals.)
    - When will I complete key tasks throughout my day?
    - Who am I going to help?

"An attitude of gratitude attracts more of what makes our lives full."

- EVENING REFLECTION: Review your goals for the week
  and the year and look back on your day.
    - What accomplishments am I proud of?
    - What am I grateful for?
    - What did I learn?
    - Was I kind to everyone today?
    - Did I procrastinate on anything really important?

This exercise will help you keep progressing in the direction that you
wish to move your life.

Chapter 9

Awesome Adventure Awaits

"Life is meant to be explored outside of our comfort zone."

ADVENTURE AWAITS EVERYWHERE ALL THE TIME

It is happening right now as we continue breathing into each change that life brings us.

Making a change today to be a better you than yesterday could be your adventure. Or perhaps today is your day to make one of the biggest dreams of your life a reality: climbing a mountain, purchasing your first home, or finding peace and happiness in this moment.

Wherever you currently are in this adventure we call life, you are where you are meant to be, right here, right now.

This is your adventure, and while it may not seem remarkable all the time, that is just a matter of personal perception.

The reality is, you are awesome.

You are uniquely you, filled with amazing stories, adventures, and moments that have brought you to this very moment.

Just take a moment to believe in yourself and your current adventure.

LIVE WILD AND FREE

Your next adventure simply requires that you be unapologetically you.

The real you. To the core.

Open your mind up to wild places and spaces where you feel the most alive.

Your wild places might be different than mine, but I wanted to share some with you that fill my life with joy.

I feel the most energized when I am spending time in the:

- Mountains
- Rivers
- Forests
- Yoga Class
- Libraries
- Coffee Shops
- Parks

I get to enjoy adventures in all these places regularly which brings me much inner joy. To me, an adventure can be as simple as walking into an unknown experience. Just because I went to the same place yesterday does not mean I will have the same experience today.

Adventure simply requires that I courageously explore life outside of my comfort zone.

While some adventures require months of training, thousands of dollars' worth of resources, and a large team, others require my ten essentials, a tank of gas, and a walk in the woods.

I've learned that life is made of both micro and macro adventures that can occur in a skate park, a local library, a coffee shop, deep in the ocean, 50 miles into the wilderness, or high in the Cascade Mountain Range.

I spend a lot of time in wild places and see far too many fellow explorers who do not bring the basic essentials that can become critical in keeping you alive. If you are an outdoor explorer, then take stock of your gear. Are you missing anything essential?

10 Essentials for Every Adventure in the Wilderness:

1. Navigation: Map and Compass
2. Skin Protection: Hat, Glasses, Sunscreen, Lip Balm & Bug Protection
3. The Right Clothes
4. Two Light Sources (headlamp + cell phone)
5. First Aid Kit + Training
6. Fire + Starters
7. Knife + Safety Training
8. Water + Purification System
9. Food: Be sure not to eat all your stores in case of an emergency.
10. Shelter: A poncho, tarp, emergency blanket or something to get out of the weather.

ACTIVITY 9.1 Make a List of Your Top Adventure Spots, Then Go!
TIME: 5-15 Minutes
SUMMARY:

- Create a list of the top 10 places that you enjoy going on adventures.
- Make time to go to one of these places in the next 24-48 hours that realistically fits into your schedule.
- Check to make sure you have all the essential gear for your next adventure.
- Additionally, consider taking this time to schedule your next big adventure, something you have always wanted to do. Refer back to your dream list from Chapter 2.

WAKE UP TO YOU.

The real you.

The authentic, happy, sad, strong, and sometimes weak human that feels and grows every single day.

Just be uniquely yourself, and fly your own freak flag. There is no need to impress anyone.

Don't be scared to open your wings and fly, share your story, and follow the next adventure that sparks your interest.

Always remember that ordinary is awesome because something extra is always within you, waiting to be ignited. Just waiting for you to define your next adventure.

It could be going on a new hike, checking out a hot spring, climbing a mountain, moving to a new town, eating at a new restaurant, asking someone to join you on your endeavors, or all of the above.

You see, adventure need not be complicated; it can really be as simple as your next breath.

YOUR NEXT ADVENTURE IS ALREADY WAITING FOR YOU

Living the life of your dreams is an adventure in and of itself. It requires action into unknown territory, and that can be scary and uncomfortable.

But it will bring you so much joy to grow, live, meet new people, and strengthen the bonds that make your life full.

Your dream life is real life. It is no longer a dream. There is no need to chase more. Continue doing the next right thing, and greatness will flow to you as a result.

MASSIVE PROGRESS

Wow, you have come a long way.

In the preceding section, you looked at communities, made a connection, and did what you could to contribute and leave a positive mark.

You connected with your life purpose and built a model for maintaining your momentum.

And finally, you planned your next adventure.

Let's break through the wall and finish.

PART FOUR:

REACH THE FINISH & SHARE YOUR GREATNESS

Chapter 10

Getting Through the Wall and Finishing

"When you hit the psychological 'wall,' STOP, BREATHE, LISTEN, and move forward into the light of the right direction."

WHAT IS THE WALL?

The wall is that voice that wants you to quit, to take the easy road and give up on your dreams.

To settle for the status quo.

That is not you.

You are meant to win the battle against the wall, to live the life your heart most desires.

THE WALLS OF LIFE

It is likely you have pushed through challenging walls in your life.

Working for years for a promotion.

Recovering from an injury.

Raising a child.

Leading a company to the next peak.

Guiding your team to the top of a mountain.

Building a life centered around your dreams.

These are all times in life when we can anticipate the wall.

Progress might start to feel like it is coming to a standstill.

At this stage of accomplishing your goals, each step might get harder, and everything and everyone may seem to be working against you.

But you keep moving because you knew this moment would come, even before you started.

ANTICIPATING "The Wall"

The energy and fire that was so alive at the starting line will begin to vanish.

It will begin to feel as though everything you do will not replenish your energy and that you cannot continue moving forward.

The pain will begin to overcome your burning desire to finish.

This is when you must rely on your community and your mental, physical, and spiritual training that carried you to this very point.

Anticipate this voice, as it will always interfere with your daily progress. It will try to win, but it never will because you will be prepared. You will know how it feels, sounds, and smells. You might even give it a name.

Even when you do not feel strong enough to continue moving forward, you will keep doing something to advance.

And with each advancement, you will get stronger, and the wall will get weaker.

ACTIVITY 10.1: Preparing for the Wall
TIME: 10 Minutes
SUMMARY:

- Envision: Close your eyes for 5 minutes and breathe as you...
  - See the wall.
  - Smell the wall.
  - Feel the wall.
  - Touch the wall.
- See yourself pushing through, climbing over, or breaking down the wall.
- Realize at which points on your journey you may experience the wall.
- Summarize: Write a summary of your vision of the wall.
- Name it. Give your wall or walls a name.

WHEN TO ANTICIPATE THE WALL

The wall will most certainly show up during every single large objective throughout life.

It might come once near the completion of something, or you may have to fight against it multiple times throughout your journey to a single outcome.

It might meet you at the starting line, at multiple points throughout your journey, and once again in the final steps.

Fortunately, this psychological battle will not last long, but it will halt progress if you stop moving.

STOPPING is when the wall gets STRONGER.

So keep moving forward.

When the voice that starts to say quit creeps in, as it always will, take a deep breath, call on your higher self, and keep moving.

If your higher self or support network are out of reach, then BELIEVE in your untapped potential. Maybe take a moment to refer back to activity 4.1 where you established belief in yourself.

Trust that you did all the prep work to get through to the finish line and win. To break down this wall and the next one.

If you do take time to stop progressing for an extended period of time, then become wary of your demons; the voice that might try to tell you to settle. They will meet you at the wall, and at some point, they might win.

When you see them coming and hear their voices, get back up and moving because they will be unprepared for you to do this, to bear victory over them. They will expect you just to sit there and stop.

TO QUIT.

So get back up, and keep moving forward.

Keep breathing.

Feel your positive energy begin to increase; feel your spirit flowing through each vein in your body.

You are winning, pushing through.

The world feels you coming, and they continue noticing your positive presence, as you build the life of your dreams.

The finish will come soon, as you begin to smell it, hear it, see it....

Keep moving and breathing. Relax into your flow.

Take it easy. And no matter how tired you are, keep moving forward.

THE FINAL STEPS

Don't stop just yet.

You can rest when you've completed the goal you set for yourself.

Enjoy these last few steps, and take a moment to reflect on all the miles you traveled to get to where you are.

Smile and breathe into your last step.

Let it go.

Leave it all at the finish line.

AT THE FINISH

You did it.

You made it through wall after wall and task after task to reach the finish.

Take the time to congratulate yourself.

Embrace this time. Soak in the positive energy from all those who surround you.

You made it through what appeared to be the impossible, and now you are a champion. Now, you can always remind yourself that just because something is challenging, it is not out of your reach.

DON'T STOP

Once you finish, don't stop moving.

Whatever you do, don't stop because your human engine will seize up.

Your momentum will slow and may eventually come to a standstill.

Keep moving because the finish is really just the beginning of your next challenge, where you will flow into a period of rest, reflection, and active recovery. This recuperation will help prevent a psychological and physical block of your natural rhythm so you can keep progressing to the next peak.

ACTIVITY 10.2: Active Finish Line Recovery
TIME: As Much Time as You Need
SUMMARY:

- Ask yourself what your mind and body most needs at this moment.
- Your needs will vary, depending on what you just accomplished. This is a great time to refer back to your health inventory from Chapter 3 for inspiration.
- Ask the people around you for the support necessary to get what your body and mind need right now.
- Micro-movements: Breathe, and softly move your entire body. Let go of all tension.
- Fuel up. Drink some water. Eat some healthy, nourishing food. Think positive thoughts. Talk positive words. Take positive actions.
- Celebrate: Most importantly, take the time to celebrate your accomplishment. Too often we do not take the time to honor our achievements in life.

CHAPTER 11

REST, REFLECT, RECOVER

"Perhaps more important than constant progress is taking time to allow your mind, body, and spirit to recover."

WHAT IS PROACTIVE REST, REFLECTION, AND RECOVERY?

Proactive rest, reflection, and recovery is honoring what your mind, body, and spirit really need to maintain a healthy state of living, so as to avoid burnout and/or debilitating pain.

THE OVERLOAD OF TODAY'S ALWAYS-ON MODE

A lot happens in a 24-hour period, let alone a week, month, year, or decade.

Too often, so much continues to happen that we fail to stop, allowing our mind, body, and spirit the necessary time to recover.

Wherever you are in life, I believe the words that follow will help guide and fuel your current and future needs to live a wholesome, balanced, and active lifestyle full of joy and laughter.

As different events arise throughout life, please allow this section to inspire your own rest, reflection, and recovery process.

Events in which you might consciously create this sacred time include the completion of a significant goal in life, such as:

- a marathon that you had trained up to for months.
- launching a new business which required consistent daily work.
- getting a promotion that you worked toward for years.
- landing a new job to support your needs.
- completing a challenging work week.
- And, most importantly when you feel the need to create a period of rest to honor your bodies health needs.

With so much going on in today's world, it is somewhat unconventional to consistently take time to rest outside of our sleep routine and look back on everything that has happened.

But this time is vital.

It allows for conscious psychological and physical recovery.

It helps us prevent overtraining, burnout, and depression, all major causes of pain.

It empowers us with the ability to keep life in balance.

While we all have a limited amount of time each day, true rest, recovery, and reflection are not something that can be rushed or limited. These vital components to life require an open-ended time frame and careful attention to what you truly need. Time should become boundless.

Because we all may be creating this period of rest for different reasons, I'd like to offer everything here as suggestions.

Let's get settled.

SETTLING INTO REST

It is time to rest.

You earned it. Your mind, body, and spirit need this vital time to recover.

Find a place and mind space of complete relaxation, a place where you feel comfortable, at ease, and most yourself. This space can be created right where you are in this moment, or you may need to move to somewhere more peaceful.

Breathe, smile, and take a moment to love yourself truly.

Embrace and honor the changes happening in life right now.

HONORING THE SACRED TIME OF RECOVERY

"In the absence of 'doing,' rest becomes sacred."

Take a moment to pause.

To do nothing.

Just breathe.

Inhale positive energy through your nose.

Exhale built up toxins through your mouth.

Just be right here, now.

Embrace the open-ended time that recovery will take.

Allow yourself the time to create sacred spaces that you will revisit during this period in life.

Perhaps you already have one location in your home or multiple places in your community.

Maybe it is right here, where you are now.

ACTIVITY 11.1: Honor Your Time of Rest
TIME: As Much Time as You Need
SUMMARY:

- Define a place or several places that can be created as sacred areas for rest, reflection, and recovery.
- Create your sacred space. Welcome candles, stones, pillows, blankets—anything you need to create a restful environment.
- Schedule time to spend in these places, or go to them when your heart is calling on you to spend some time there.
- Getting settled in your space…
  - Make yourself comfortable. Comfort is key.
  - Close your eyes for a moment and focus on your breath.
  - Again, close your eyes and listen to what your body needs. Your body is already telling your mind what you need. Write your needs down in your notebook.

Adapt this time to what you truly need. It might be sleep, nutrition, and a short break from what you are working on.

Or, perhaps your body is calling for days, weeks, or even months of recovery because you have been pushing it athletically and/or professionally for years.

Take a moment to breathe into a smile.

Congratulate yourself on all the progress you've made on your journey.

It is time to REST. To allow your body some vital time to gather strength before reflecting on the miles you have traveled to get to where you are.

Proper rest requires….
- **Relaxation** to free your mind and body from tension.
- **Energy** to fuel your bodies restorative functions.
- **Solitude** to empower you with an environment of peace.
- **Time** to become boundless.

Rest enables your body's cellular, musculoskeletal, psychological, and spiritual makeup to recover. It brings you back to a balanced state of being. It is vital for your survival and ability to continue on your path of happiness and prosperity.

Allow your rest to be as long as it needs to be. Sometimes, this will be minutes, while at other times, you may need hours, days, weeks, or months to recover to a stable state of being so you can start on your next primary objective in life.

As you rest, allow new energy to flow into you, and let go of your past. Let go of what you are holding on to in your mind, body, and spirit.

During this time, your body will be working to get stronger. To re-build what has been broken, using new pieces of you. Because you have changed. You are not the same person as you were yesterday, last week, month, or year. On the outside, you may appear to be the same person, but on the inside, you are changing with each breath of life and each action moving you forward. You are stronger, more mindful, and more in tune with the person you want to be.

Remember, this process of rest will take time, as much time as you need. As you spend this time in rest, allow for transitions to naturally occur as they always have.

If you are sick, then allow your body to rest purely. Do not set the alarm or watch TV; just breathe into a calm state of being.

Use this time to go back to the health tune-up section and take an inventory. This could take as little as 5 minutes, yet it may be the key to showing you exactly what your body needs.

Your body is likely demanding some combination of healthy, nour-ishing relationships, sleep, nutrition, and relaxation.

Use this time to open your mind to new sources of inspiration and new methods of healing.

Welcome new books into this time, start some art projects, visit new places, and experience new forms of rest therapy such as 50+ yoga classes, swimming, meditation, quality sleep, nutrition, and most importantly, holistic self-care.

LOOKING BACK TO HOW WE GOT HERE

Reflection gives us the opportunity to honor our progress, no matter how big or small it is, as well as identify what we wish to continue doing and what we want to change.

Take time to look back on your progress in all aspects of life.

No matter how big or small, you have made some form of progress in all areas that make your life full.

ACTIVITY 11.2: Complete a Personal Reflection
TIME: 10-15 Minutes
SUMMARY:

- What have you done in the following key areas to improve the quality of life you get to live today? It may be as simple as helping a stranger, learning a micro-skill, or starting a short meditation practice.
  - Health_____
  - Community_____
  - Career_____
  - Relationships_____
  - Spirituality_____
  - Personal Growth_____
  - Finance_____
  - Adventure_____
- What do you wish to change in your life?
- What are you going to continue doing or re-commit to?

EVERYDAY PROGRESS

Whether you believe it or not right now, you have done something to move your entire life forward.

The changes in your life have likely not been easy, but they most certainly have been worthwhile. Each day that you make progress, your life becomes a little more aligned with who you truly want to be. With the freedom, peace, and happiness you deserve.

In your reflection, look back at where you started this journey and where you are now.

What change in life are you most proud of as a result of the work you have done?

If needed, take the time to sit with this question for a few minutes or even a few days. Think carefully before writing down what you are most proud of. This will help you create more of these kinds of changes in your life as you flow forward.

THE POWER OF NO

"Say yes less and experience less stress."

Yes brings new opportunities to life, but equally powerful is the word no, especially when we have said yes to too many things.

Practice a healthy balance of saying yes to the right things that support your life and no to the things that might be holding you back from completing what you are destined to do.

ACTIVITY 11.3: Rebalance the Scales and Let Go
TIME: 30 Minutes
SUMMARY:

- Now, ponder the following question as you enjoy a short walk before returning to write out your answer.
- What do you need to begin saying no to in order to become more aligned with your "Life on Purpose" and/or the completion of your major goals in life? Remember, these items will help support a healthier, happier, and more inspiring you.
  1. _____
  2. _____
  3. _____
- Complete the table below or in your notebook by rewriting the three things you are going to stop, when you will stop them, and your next step to do so.

The Thing I Need to Stop	When I Will Stop	Next Step

LETTING GO CREATES SPACE FOR NEW GROWTH

During this stage of your growth, allow yourself time to do the hard work of letting go of things that distract you from what your heart most desires. This is not easy, but it is always worth it.

Embrace your progress. Feel your feelings. Continue helping others. Continue living your life on purpose.

And, whatever you do, show up to BE the greatest YOU every day.

CHAPTER 12

SHARE YOUR STORY

"Within all of us, there lies experiences that have the power to uplift the world."

THE STORY WITHIN YOU

You, like me, have stories to share.

Your experiences could be the spark to inspire positive change in your family, friendships, company, school, community, and country.

Your words could support people who need a new map and compass to redirect their life in the direction that sings most true to their heart.

Whether you believe it or not, you have a story that has the power to change people's lives, including your own.

You could have the power to inspire someone to make a scary change in life; to prevent or provide a solution to suicide, drug, and alcohol addiction; to bring people together to support community service projects, and so much more. Your story will ultimately help make this world a happier, healthier, and safer place for all beings to prosper.

So, start sharing your story today.

BUILDING THE COURAGE TO SPEAK

Let go of your fear of speaking up because, in speaking, you actually have the power to help others.

Fear of rejection or other people's opinions of us often blocks our voice. Allow speaking to become an action you take to break these false fears.

The simple fact of life is that not everyone will be receptive to what you have to share, and at some point, someone likely told you this openly. This feedback can create an ongoing fear of always being rejected. Shatter this fear by continuing to share your story with those who are willing to listen.

Speak up and share your greatness.

Let your thoughts and experiences improve the world, your community, and the relationships that matter most to you. Create the time to look back on your life, reflect on your proudest moments, and learn lessons from both the good and bad times. Share these lessons with others.

BREATHE THROUGH YOUR WORDS

As you begin to share, speak slowly, and create space to breathe.

One word and sentence at a time, one breath at a time.

Let your story naturally flow.

BELIEVE YOU HAVE SOMETHING TO BE PROUD OF

It starts with a simple belief that everything you have done in life up to this point matters.

Believe that in sharing your experience, you are helping others who may have traveled through similar life experiences.

But always remember to THINK before speaking up…

Is it the truth? Is it honest, inspiring, necessary, and kind?

This simple pause and reflection can help gauge whether our stories should be shared openly or in a different context.

MOST EVERYTHING IS WORTH SHARING

The good, great, bad, and ugly make you who you are today.

High points and low points in life are essential to completing your story.

Each experience brought you to this moment, this breath, this day.

Share your successes, your failures, the things you are most proud of, and the moments you wish you could change. Let these all go. In doing so, you will naturally open up space for new experiences.

Share all of yourself. Do not hide the details of the pain you may have traveled through. You may want to make yourself sound larger than life, but the truth is, we all struggle through each success and failure. That is just a simple fact of life.

In sharing, be honest, open, willing, and loving. Be you.

FREEDOM IN SHARING

You will most certainly find freedom and new energy in sharing your experiences from life. And, you will soon realize that what you have to say really does matter.

No longer will old thoughts and experiences be stored in your brain, taking up vital space.

You will open up space to allow new thoughts, ideas, and energy into your life.

Relief will wash over you as if you had dropped a fifty-pound backpack after miles of hiking.

Also, always remember that in not sharing, our ego is actually inflated because we are focused on "little old me." We are stuck in fear and unable to free ourselves from the bondage of self that prevents progress.

WE LEARN TO LISTEN

In sharing, we actually learn to listen. This is because sharing creates a welcoming environment for honest, open, and constructive conversations with others.

It allows us to learn from both our experiences and the experiences of others in our communities. The new employee, student, friend, person on the street—they all have something to teach us if only we are willing to open a space for sharing.

However, in sharing conversation and stories with others, strive not become a "me monster" who is solely focused on the self and not welcoming comments and inspiring conversation. Do not shut out someone's voice, since you may find inspiration in listening to others.

BE THE 25% TALKER

A 25% talker is someone who shares 25% of the time and, in doing so, inspires others to share for the other 75%.

This enables you to become a power listener, someone who is sought after for advice, insight, and feedback. Someone people trust and feel comfortable sharing around. You actually empower others by listening.

And, if you listen for long enough, you will often hear your own thoughts, and ideas shared by someone else.

SHARING IS CARING

Always remember that you have a voice and that what you say matters.

Take the time to reflect on your experiences in life.

Write about them, talk about them, and share them. In doing so you will most certainly help others.

And, like a butterfly, let your words freely take flight.

Let them flow,

Day and night,

Give them time to grow,

And always, always know,

What you have to share matters.

ACTIVITY 12.1: Share Your Experience
TIME: To Be Personally Defined
SUMMARY:

- Identify a short story or longer experience that you would be willing to share with others.
- Write or record your experience.
- Use the questions below to inspire the structure of your story.
  - Where were you?
  - What happened?
  - What did you learn?
  - Who was part of it?
  - How did it change you?
  - How did it make you feel?
  - Would you do it again?
  - How would you improve the situational outcome?
- Share It:
  - Pick a close friend, mentor, family member, or colleague to share your experience with.
  - Create an environment where you feel comfortable sharing your story.
  - Most importantly, as you share your story with others, create an open, two-way dialogue.

THE END... IS ONLY THE BEGINNING

"Perhaps now is not the end, but merely the end of a new beginning."

Welcome to the end, where we might think our work is done, but it has really only just begun.

AS YOU MOVE FORWARD FROM HERE ALWAYS REMEMBER TO...

Find focus through breath.

Keep dreaming big dreams.

Focus on health, your greatest wealth.

Set goals and gain clarity on a vision for your life.

Find joy in your journey.

With community, you are stronger than alone.

A life on purpose is full of joy.

Keep moving forward one step at a time.

Adventures are quite literally waiting everywhere.

Finishing what we started is better than leaving things undone.

Rest is often best at the end of an accomplishment in life or when your body most needs it.

Sharing is caring.

Aim to always look at the end of one experience in life merely as the beginning of a new one.

A NEW BEGINNING

I'd like to thank you for allowing me to become a part of your path toward realizing the life of your dreams.

While our journey here is nearing an end, I'd like us to look at it merely as the beginning of a new chapter on this adventure through life.

I'd like to offer this meditation about endings and beginnings.

THE ENDING MEDITATION

Close your eyes and focus on the progress you have made during your journey through this book. Nothing more.

....

Open your eyes to the whole new world, just waiting for your greatness.

Take a moment to look around at all the beauty that naturally rests in your presence.

Breathe in....

....

Breathe out....

....

Breathe in....

....

Breathe out....

....

Lightly hold all of the words, exercises, and work that you have completed during this book.

Breathe in....

....

Breathe out....

....

Kindly look at all the change, progress, and actions you have taken to become the whole person you are right now in this moment.

Breathe in....

....

Breathe out....

....

Feel your heart pounding inside as you begin to prepare for the opening of a new door in your life.

Breathe in....

....

Breathe out....

....

Open the door to your new beginning with this next breath.

NOW IS NO TIME TO STOP WHAT YOU HAVE BUILT ON THIS JOURNEY

Continue taking massive action, maintaining your newly-found momentum, and living your life on purpose every single day.

Learn from your experiences and share them with others.

Most importantly, always stay true to yourself and honor your daily growth and progress.

Remind yourself that you are perfect as you are right now in this moment.

A new chapter, a new way of life, and a new you have taken flight.

As you travel forward, may you continue to fill your heart with what it most longs for.

Until our paths cross again on the next summit in life, I wish you a healthy, balanced, and active lifestyle; strong community connections; joyful living; safe and amazing adventures; a heart full of gratitude; personal and professional growth; and healthy, loving relationships.

See You on the Summit,
Scott ^ :)

ABOUT THE AUTHOR

When he was 29, Scott had a profound inner awakening that redirected the course of his life, inspiring him to write his first book; BRIDGE in which he shares many of the frameworks he used to transform his life completely.

During his inner transformation, Scott connected with his primary purpose; to use his adventurous spirit and passion for personal excellence to inspire and empower people, communities, and businesses around the world.

Spiritual growth, adventure photography, coaching, writing, global exploration, and entrepreneurship provide Scott with channels to live his life on purpose, deliver a positive message, and inspire others to realize their dreams.

His education is from Oregon State University in Entrepreneurship and International Business. Scott is the co-founder of Peak Prosper; a socially and environmentally conscious company on a mission to have a positive impact on one-million people around the world.

Exploring new and unknown territory in the mountains and business inspires Scott. It fuels his internal drive to wake up each day and make everything better than the last. When not working on books, consulting projects, and business development you will find Scott exploring wild places in remote areas of the world, or exploring his backyard of Mt. Hood, Oregon.

Based out of Hood River, Oregon, USA, Scott continues to write about his experiences in business and the great outdoors to continue making our world a better place.

scottrowley.com

Peak Prosper exists to deliver world-class products and experiences that inspire & empower people with resources to realize the life of their dreams.

We are a socially, and environmentally conscious company who strives to live the principles presented in our products as part of our business and lifestyles. We carry out our promise to make this world a better place by providing many free resources, donating 12% of our net sales to our giveback partners, and remaining active in our communities. Additionally, each product and service developed at Peak Prosper is done so to live our core values of health, community, and adventure.

We believe every one of us is on this planet to enjoy life to the fullest, to find meaning and purpose in our being, and to live the life of our dreams. That is why we started Peak Prosper. To provide you with the tools, resources, and inspiration to build a life that you are genuinely excited to lead every day.

Additional products and resources are available online at peakprosper.com.

Peak Prosper, Inc.

peakprosper.com

info@peakprosper.com

Made in the USA
San Bernardino, CA
15 November 2018